# THIS BO[obscured] BELONGS TO...

| Name: | Age: |
|---|---|

| Favourite player: |
|---|

## 2021/2022

| My Predictions... | Actual... |
|---|---|
| Town's final position: | |
| | |
| Town's top scorer: | |
| | |
| League One winners: | |
| | |
| League One top scorer: | |
| | |
| FA Cup winners: | |
| | |
| EFL Cup winners: | |
| | |

Contributors: Peter Rogers

## A TWOCAN PUBLICATION



ISBN: 978-1-913362-95-9

**PICTURE CREDITS:** Match Day Images, Paul Macro, Action Images, Alamy and Press Association.

**£9**

IPSWICH TOWN
FOOTBALL CLUB

# CONTENTS

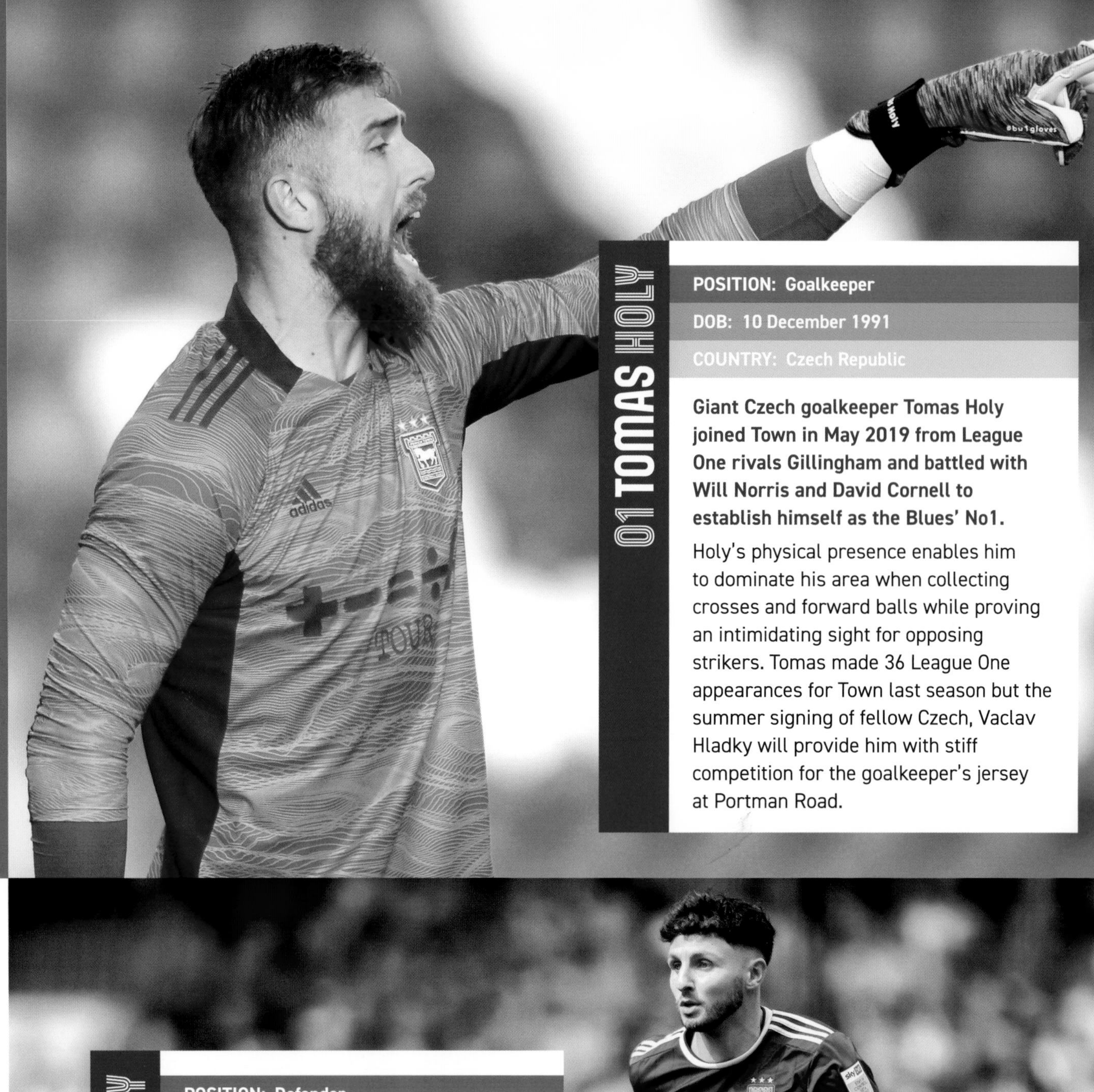


## 01 TOMAS HOLY

**POSITION:** Goalkeeper

**DOB:** 10 December 1991

**COUNTRY:** Czech Republic

**Giant Czech goalkeeper Tomas Holy joined Town in May 2019 from League One rivals Gillingham and battled with Will Norris and David Cornell to establish himself as the Blues' No1.**

Holy's physical presence enables him to dominate his area when collecting crosses and forward balls while proving an intimidating sight for opposing strikers. Tomas made 36 League One appearances for Town last season but the summer signing of fellow Czech, Vaclav Hladky will provide him with stiff competition for the goalkeeper's jersey at Portman Road.

## 03 MATT PENNEY

**POSITION:** Defender

**DOB:** 11 February 1998

**COUNTRY:** England

**A free agent in the summer of 2021 following his release from Sheffield Wednesday, Matt Penney agreed a two-year deal at Portman Road on 29 June.**

With the ability to operate at left-back or in a more advanced role in midfield, Penney's versatility looks set to make him a valuable member of the Town squad. The 23-year-old played 32 games for the Owls and also had loan spells with Bradford City and Mansfield Town before spending the 2019/20 season in Germany with St Pauli.

# SQUAD

# 2021/22

## 04 REKEEM HARPER

**POSITION:** Midfielder

**DOB:** 8 March 2000

**COUNTRY:** England

**A product of the West Bromwich Albion Academy, all-action midfielder Rekeem Harper joined Ipswich Town on a three-year deal in June 2021.**

The midfielder had a brief taste of Premier League football at the Hawthorns and also has valuable experience of League One and the Championship to call upon following loan spells at Blackburn Rovers and Birmingham City. The 21-year-old is expected to be a key man in Town's 2021/22 campaign.

# JANOI DONACIEN

**The side-foot pass is one of the most accurate passing techniques over shorter distances. The ability to find one of your teammates with a pass, even when under severe pressure, and retain possession of the ball is an essential factor in the way the game is played today.**

# SIDE-FOOT PASS

# SOCCER SKILLS

## EXERCISE ONE

Set up a 10 x 10m grid. In one corner there are two players and on each of the other three corners there is one player.

Player A starts with the ball. Each player must pass the ball round the square in sequence then follow their pass. A passes to B then runs after his pass and takes up B's starting position. B passes to C and follows his pass to take C's position, and so on. All of the players must control the ball then pass it with the inside of their foot.

### Key Factors

1. **Non-kicking foot alongside the ball.**
2. **Pass with the inside of the foot.**
3. **Strike through the middle of the ball.**
4. **Keep your eyes on the ball and your head steady.**

## EXERCISE TWO

The set up is the same as exercise one.

In this exercise the players pass the ball in sequence, A through to D, but do not follow their pass, remaining stationary.

As soon as A plays the first pass, E sets off racing around the outside of the starting point. The players must pass the ball as quickly and accurately as possible while under pressure from E, who cannot tackle but is effectively racing the ball round the square.

The same key factors apply in this exercise as in the first, but the players are required to be able to pass the ball accurately while under pressure.

**Any team who can retain possession through good accurate passing will always make it very difficult for the opposition. The side-foot pass is one of the most accurate passing techniques.**

# JOHN WARK

# TOWN HEROES

**Town legend John Wark amassed a total of 678 appearances for the Blues, 670 starts and eight substitute appearances, over three separate spells at Portman Road.**

Born in Glasgow, Wark was a goalscoring midfielder who progressed through the youth and reserve ranks to become a real star performer during the club's golden era under the management of Bobby Robson.

**A member of Town's 1978 FA Cup winning team, Wark's goals were the catalyst for the club's UEFA Cup triumph in 1981. He scored 14 goals in the competition including one in each leg of the final as Town overcame Dutch side AZ Alkmaar 5-4 on aggregate.**

## ENCOURAGEMENT

As an experienced member of the Ipswich side, Wark's words of advice, wisdom and encouragement were of great benefit to younger members of the Town team - this particularly became the case in his latter years at Portman Road.

## VISION

Wark was blessed with great vision on the pitch, he had an excellent ability to spot teammate's runs and his eye for accuracy was often used to perfection when he orchestrated set-piece situations too.

## ENERGY

A true box-to-box midfielder who consistently demonstrated great energy levels. Wark's lungs must have worked overtime on a matchday as he set off on many powerful forward runs from midfield to support the Town attack.

## GOALS

Wark scored an impressive 179 goals for Ipswich Town and the majority came from his trusty right foot. Sometimes struck from distance and often confidently dispatched from the penalty spot too. When Wark pulled the trigger, his right foot rarely let him down.

**ALL OF THESE FOOTY TERMS ARE HIDDEN IN THE GRID, EXCEPT FOR ONE... CAN YOU WORK OUT WHICH ONE?**

| A | G | F | G | O | L | D | E | N | G | O | A | L | A | A | V | [illegible] | [illegible] | [illegible] | [illegible] |
|---|---|---|---|---|---|---|---|---|---|---|---|---|---|---|---|---|---|---|---|
| O | C | L | E | A | N | S | H | E | E | T | N | T | X | O | A | [illegible] | [illegible] | [illegible] | [illegible] |
| D | R | I | B | B | L | I | N | G | A | Y | H | B | L | U | C | [illegible] | [illegible] | [illegible] | [illegible] |
| E | B | P | H | R | N | R | U | T | F | F | Y | U | R | C | V | [illegible] | [illegible] | [illegible] | [illegible] |
| A | F | F | H | I | T | T | H | E | W | O | O | D | W | O | R | K | [illegible] | [illegible] | G |
| D | I | L | C | E | N | S | X | D | T | V | R | C | G | R | G | E | O | T | S |
| B | M | A | D | J | P | Z | E | U | I | W | J | F | N | E | A | D | E | Z | M |
| A | R | P | K | U | L | I | E | F | S | B | M | A | M | P | I | K | O | S | R |
| L | Q | A | T | A | T | M | S | D | O | E | M | T | R | P | J | P | Q | P | A |
| L | Y | V | C | P | O | A | G | O | I | D | U | A | A | I | Y | T | N | B | I |
| S | I | W | U | E | T | G | T | A | R | N | V | B | T | K | A | H | V | W | N |
| P | R | C | L | I | N | I | C | A | L | F | I | N | I | S | H | E | R | N | B |
| E | R | Z | N | S | T | C | H | X | M | A | M | A | M | I | E | N | L | A | O |
| C | Q | E | H | C | N | S | H | Y | O | S | U | J | G | L | T | U | E | M | W |
| I | O | A | F | O | S | P | T | E | W | R | O | D | B | Z | A | M | X | T | K |
| A | J | I | N | F | F | O | X | I | N | T | H | E | B | O | X | B | F | E | I |
| L | K | A | D | E | A | N | T | Y | V | N | R | K | B | S | Q | I | C | G | C |
| I | M | G | F | M | U | G | I | A | N | T | K | I | L | L | I | N | G | R | K |
| S | X | P | B | U | H | E | L | G | L | O | R | T | N | O | C | L | L | A | B |
| T | H | E | B | E | A | U | T | I | F | U | L | G | A | M | E | S | P | T | T |

# SOCCER SEARCH

Ball Control
Bicycle Kick
Boot it
Brace
Clean Sheet

Clinical Finisher
Cruyff Turn
Cup-tied
Dead-ball Specialist
Dribbling

Flip Flap
Fox in the Box
Gaffer
Giant-killing
Golden Goal

Hard Man
Hit the Woodwork
Magic Sponge
Man On
Nutmeg

Rainbow Kick
Skipper
Target Man
The Beautiful Game
Treble

ANSWERS ON PAGE 62

## 05 GEORGE EDMUNDSON

**POSITION:** Defender

**DOB:** 15 August 1997

**COUNTRY:** England

**Central defender George Edmundson joined Town in July 2021 from Scottish Premier League champions Glasgow Rangers and agreed a four-year deal at Portman Road.**

Born in Manchester, the 24-year-old began his career with Oldham Athletic before heading north of the border in the summer of 2019. Edmundson played on loan at Derby County last season and following the departures of Luke Chambers and James Wilson from the Blues squad, he will be keen to establish himself in a new-look Ipswich defence.

## 06 LUKE WOOLFENDEN

**POSITION:** Defender

**DOB:** 21 October 1998

**COUNTRY:** England

**A product of the Town Academy set-up, Ipswich-born Luke Woolfenden is a confident defender who is calm in possession and swift to spot danger from opposing forwards.**

After gaining valuable first-team experience with a loan spell at Swindon Town in 2018/19, Woolfenden returned to Town and agreed a new four-year contract at Portman Road in the summer of 2020 - he appears set to be a mainstay of the Blues defence for many seasons to come.

# SQUAD 2021/22

## 07 WES BURNS

**POSITION:** Midfielder

**DOB:** 23 November 1994

**COUNTRY:** Wales

**Attacking midfielder Wes Burns became Town's first summer signing when joined the club on 3 June 2021.**

After scoring 23 goals in 176 games for Fleetwood Town, Burns joined Ipswich from their League One rivals for an undisclosed fee having made a positive impression in the Cod Army's two games against Ipswich in 2020/21. An attacking right-sided midfielder, the Welshman will be looking to create chances for others and weigh in with goals too in the Blues' 2021/22 League One campaign.

There are five Blueys hiding in the crowd as fans celebrate the Tractor Boys bringing home the UEFA Cup in 1981.

## Can you find him?

ANSWERS ON PAGE 62

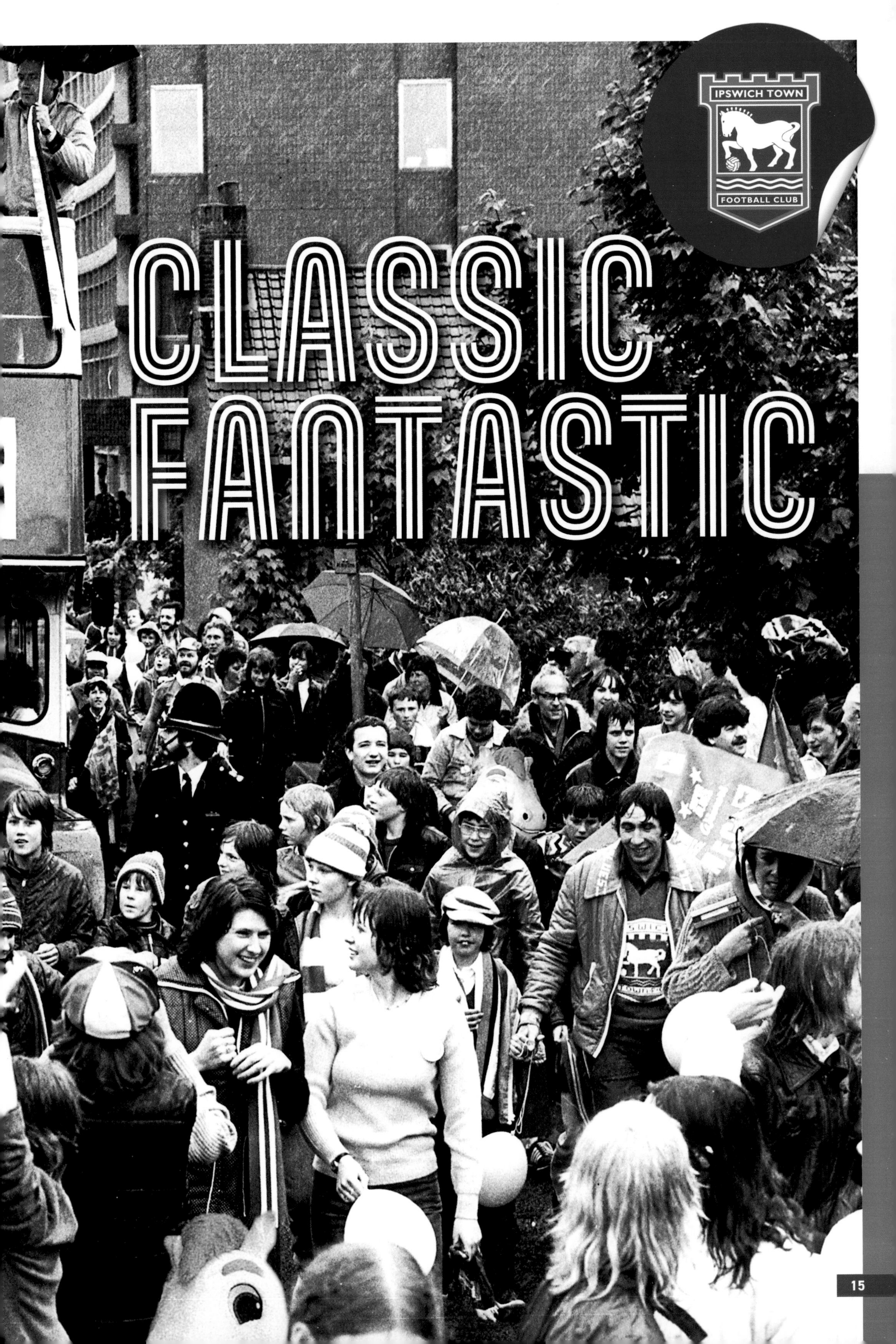
IPSWICH TOWN
FOOTBALL CLUB
CLASSIC
FANTASTIC

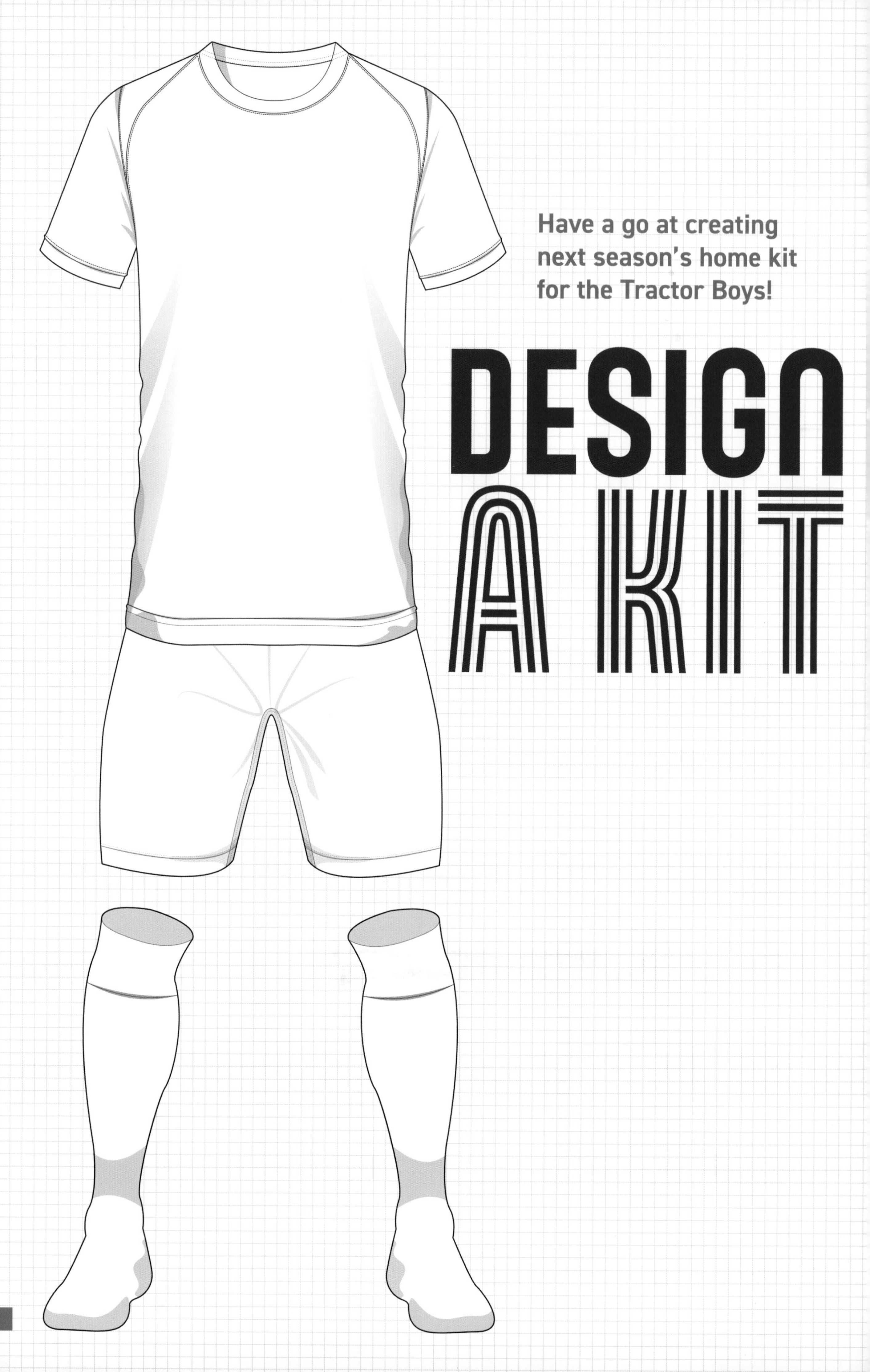

Have a go at creating next season's home kit for the Tractor Boys!

# DESIGN A KIT

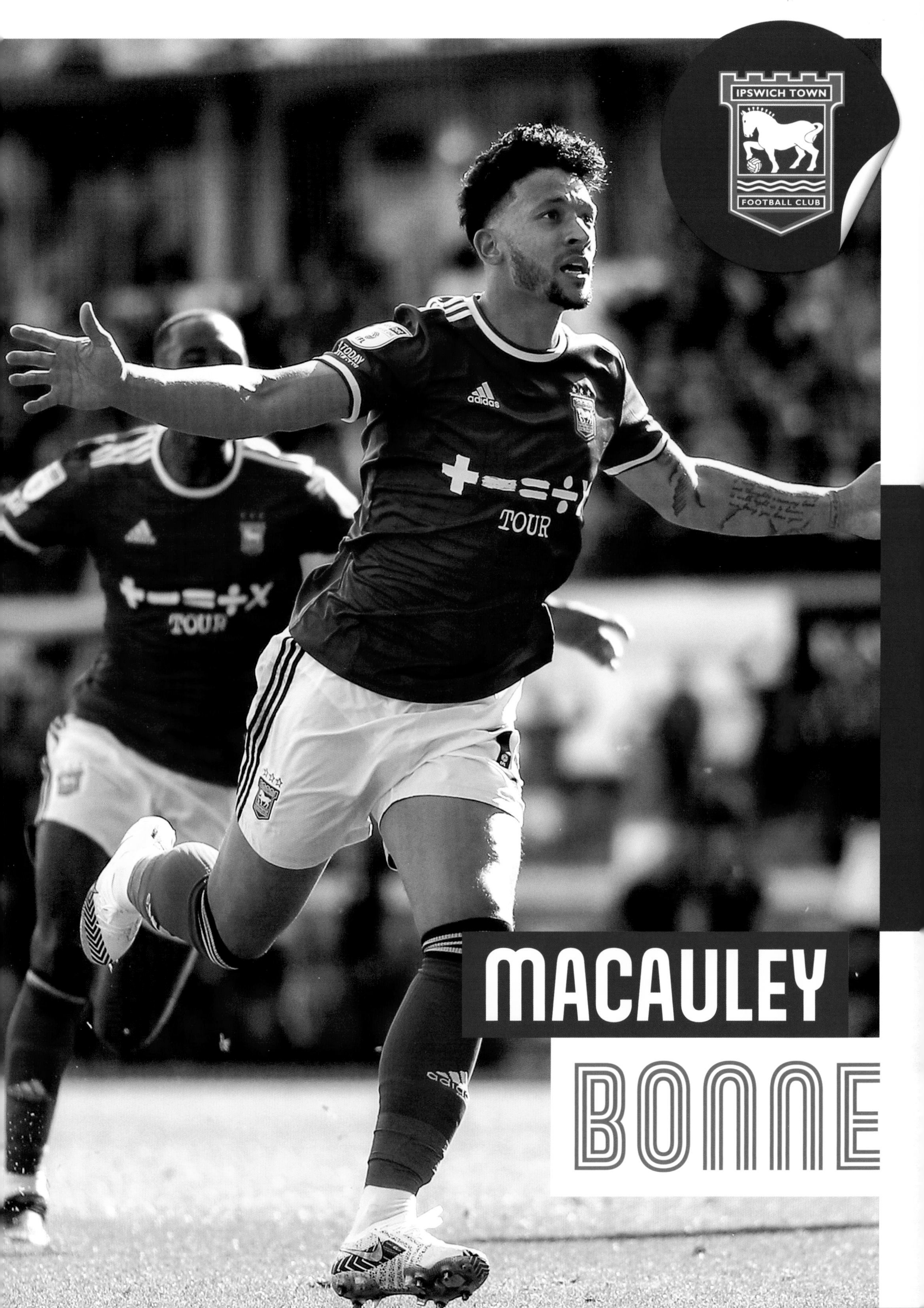


# MACAULEY BONNE

Town's blue shirts, white shorts and blue socks have been a long held tradition at Portman Road. However, excitement and anticipation still surround every new Ipswich Town kit.

Each and every playing strip forms its own part of Ipswich Town history and supporters young and old will all have their own favourites. Let's take a look back at some of the best...

# 1980/81

**A strip synonymous with the club's 1980/81 UEFA Cup triumph, Town's classic Adidas kit from the late '70s and early '80s brings back memories of the club's halcyon days under the management of Bobby Robson.**

A classic blue shirt with white collar and three Adidas stripes on the sleeves, the shirt also carried the manufacturer's logo and club crest. The brilliant white shorts complete with three blue stripes on the side and Adidas logo were capped off by blue socks complete with three white stripes at the top.

For many supporters this really is the kit that all Town kits are judged by. Of course the club enjoyed great success in this strip but win, lose or draw this look really is classic Ipswich Town. Unsurprisingly, as the club acknowledged the 40th anniversary of the 1980/81 UEFA Cup success in 2020/21, the home kit was designed to replicate this club classic.

## DRESSED TO IMPRESS

**Town produced a sensational display in this kit as they engineered a 3-0 victory over AZ Alkmaar at Portman Road in the first leg of the UEFA Cup final on 6 May 1981. Goals from John Wark, Frans Thijssen and Paul Mariner provided Bobby Robson's men with the platform to lift the trophy in Amsterdam a fortnight later.**

## HE WORE IT WELL

Signed from FC Twente for £150,000 back in the summer of 1978, Dutch midfielder Arnold Muhren wore this kit with great distinction. While donning this classic Town shirt, Muhren wowed the Portman Road faithful with his impressive array of passing skills. Blessed with a wand of a left foot, Muhren was the creator of many goals for ace marksman Alan Brazil after the two men created a great on-pitch understanding.

**Having won promotion to the inaugural Premier League in 1992, Umbro produced a new look for Town that was certainly befitting of the Premier League's 'whole new ball game' image.**

Complete with white sleeves, this new look shirt included a retro style lace-up collar with red lacing sitting on the traditional white collar. The main body of the shirt was of course Ipswich's traditional blue with the kit manufacturer's logo, club sponsor and Town badge on a red background all housed on the front of the shirt.

The white shorts had a red and blue trim with the Umbro logo and also included the Town badge which was again mounted on a red shield to marry up with the shirt. The blue socks had a white band at the top which also carried a red trim.

## DRESSED TO IMPRESS

**When Town began life in the Premier League with an opening-day match against Aston Villa on 15 August 1992, their lace-up collar look was matched by the visitors whose own Umbro kit also carried this stylish look.**

The bright white sleeves looked highly impressive on a sun drenched afternoon at Portman Road. Town's new strip certainly looked easy on the eye and the team's football matched. An impressive first-half display was rewarded with a memorable long-range strike from Gavin Johnson before Ipswich old boy Dalian Atkinson levelled late on for Villa.

## HE WORE IT WELL

Local hero Jason Dozzell always looked at home in any Town shirt but he certainly produced some of his best performances in this classic Town kit. Dozzell featured in 41 Premier League matches in 1992/93 and netted seven league goals including a brace in the 3-1 East Anglian derby victory over Norwich City at Portman Road in April 1993.

## 1992/93

# ALL KITTED OUT

## 08 LEE EVANS

**POSITION:** Midfielder

**DOB:** 24 July 1994

**COUNTRY:** Wales

**Former Wigan Athletic midfielder Lee Evans linked up with his former Latics boss Paul Cook when he agreed a three-year deal at Portman Road in June 2021.**

Capped on four occasions by the Wales national team, the Newport-born midfielder played a vital role in the Latics' League One survival last season and his vast experience looks all set to bring some real knowhow to the Town midfield.

## 09 JOE PIGOTT

**POSITION:** Striker

**DOB:** 24 November 1993

**COUNTRY:** England

**Striker Joe Pigott netted 20 goals at League One level last season for AFC Wimbledon and will be keen to continue his hot streak at Portman Road after agreeing a three-year deal with Town in July 2021.**

The 6ft 2in frontman began his career with Charlton Athletic and after a host of loan moves and a spell in non-league football, he excelled at Wimbledon where he boasted a record of 54 goals in 157 appearances for the London club.

# SQUAD 2021/22

## 10 JAMES NORWOOD

POSITION: Striker
DOB: 5 September 1990
COUNTRY: England

**Following a goal-laden four-season spell with Tranmere Rovers, striker James Norwood joined Ipswich Town in the summer of 2019.**

The livewire frontman netted eleven League One goals in his first season at Portman Road and hit double figures in all competitions again in 2020/21 despite an injury-hit campaign. A fully fit James Norwood is expected to be right among the goals again for Paul Cook's men in 2021/22.

## 11 SCOTT FRASER

POSITION: Midfielder
DOB: 30 March 1995
COUNTRY: Scotland

**Goalscoring midfielder Scott Fraser became Ipswich Town's eighth signing of a hectic summer transfer window as Paul Cook rebuilt the Blues squad ahead of the 2021/22 League One campaign.**

Fraser was a standout performer in League One last season and his arrival from MK Dons was seen as a real coup for Town. With the ability to score goals and create chances for others, Scott is sure to have the Portman Road crowd up and off their feet over the coming season.

**Keeping fit and healthy is vital for all of us. So if you play footy for the school team or your local club, being fit and ready for action is sure to help you enjoy the game and perform to your very best.**

For the players at Ipswich Town, showing peak levels of fitness is essential if they want to feature in Paul Cook's team. Before anyone can think of pulling on the famous blue shirt and taking to the pitch at Portman Road on a Saturday afternoon, they will have had to perform well in training at Playford Road and to have shown the manager, his coaches and fitness staff that they are fully fit and ready for the physical challenges that await them on a matchday.

Regardless of whether training takes place at the training ground or at the stadium, the players' fitness remains an all-important factor.

Of course, time spent working on training drills and playing small-sided games will help a player's fitness, but there is lots of work undertaken just to ensure maximum levels of fitness are reached. Away from the training pitches the professional players will spend a great deal of time in the gymnasium partaking in their own personal workouts. Bikes, treadmills and weights will all form part of helping the players reach and maintain a top level of fitness.

**Over the course of a week the players will take part in many warm-up and aerobic sessions and even complete yoga and pilates classes to help with core strength and general fitness. The strength and conditioning coaches at the club work tirelessly to do all they can to make sure that the Ipswich Town players you see in action on a matchday really are fighting fit for footy!**

# GET FIT FOR FOOTY

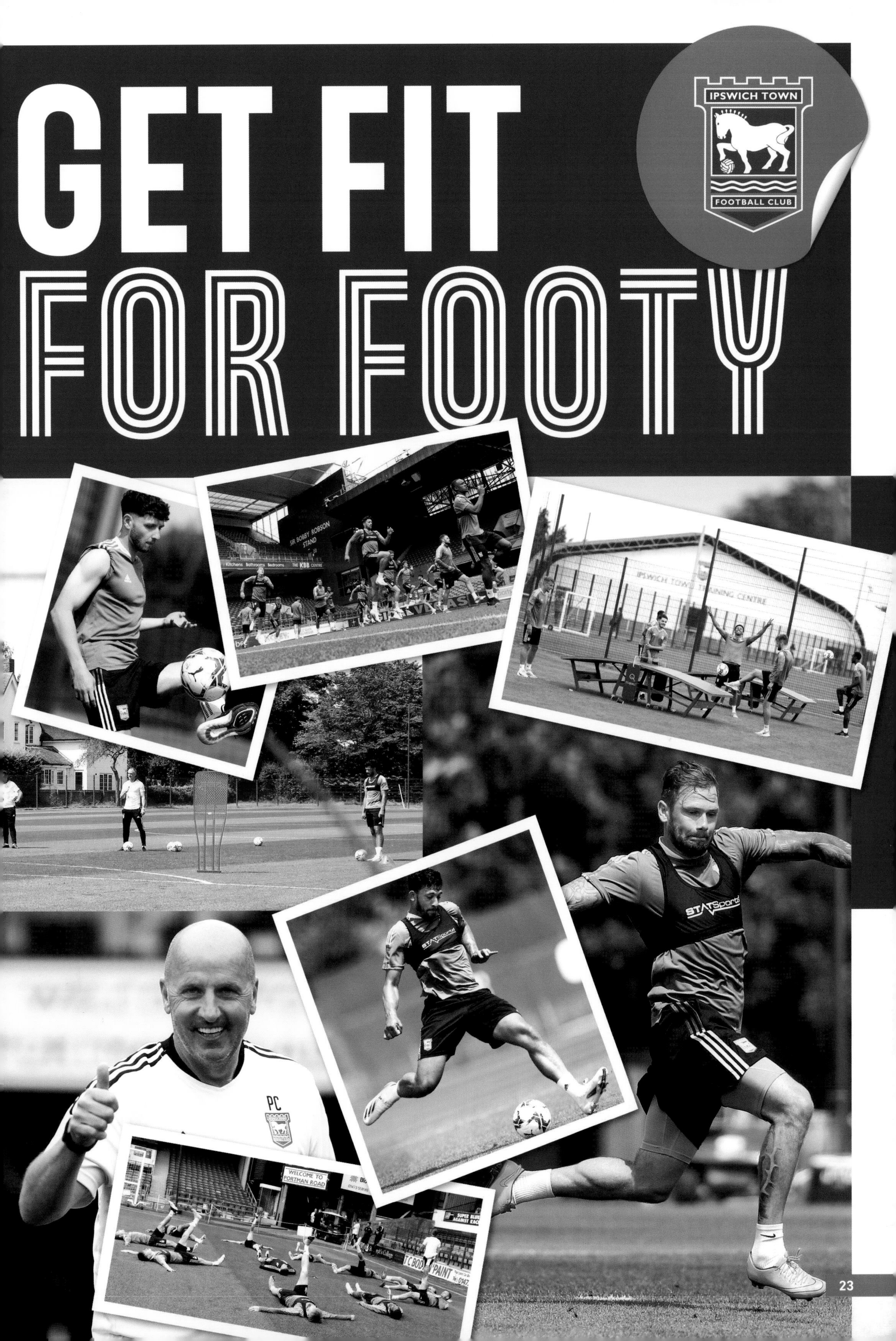

# KYLE EDWARDS

It has been said that dribbling is a dying art. The pace of the modern game makes it more difficult, but there are players about, even in today's lightning fast conditions, who have the confidence to keep hold of the ball and take on defenders.

# DRIBBLING

# SOCCER SKILLS

## EXERCISE ONE

As a warm-up exercise, players A and B each dribble a ball around a 20 x 10m grid, avoiding each other, but staying within the grid boundary lines.

They progress to a 'cat and mouse' race between the corners - the player with the most visits to each corner wins the race. One of the main problems in this exercise is avoiding the other player, and their ball.

## EXERCISE TWO

Now for a more realistic exercise. Six players are used as shown, with three attackers and three defenders at any one time. When play starts, the players with the ball attack any of the three opposing goals, changing their target as they choose. The defenders have, simply, to stop their opposite number from scoring, but must not interfere with any other pair.

## Key Factors

1. **Close control.**
2. **Quick change of direction.**
3. **Acceleration away from defender.**
4. **Feints, to wrong-foot defender.**
5. **Head up to see the whole picture.**

When the defenders win possession, they become the attackers, and go for goal themselves. This can be a very enjoyable practice, but also quite tiring.

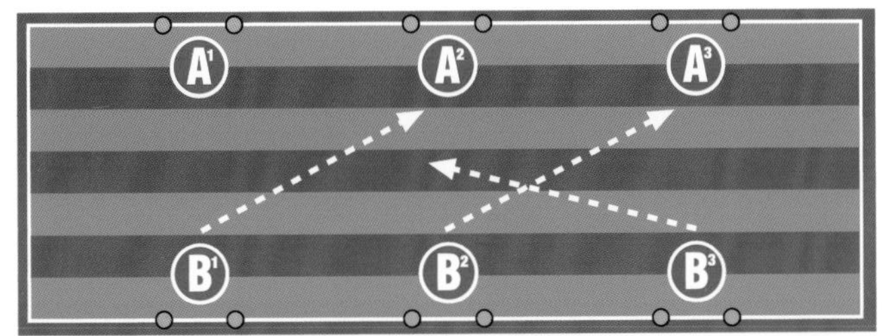

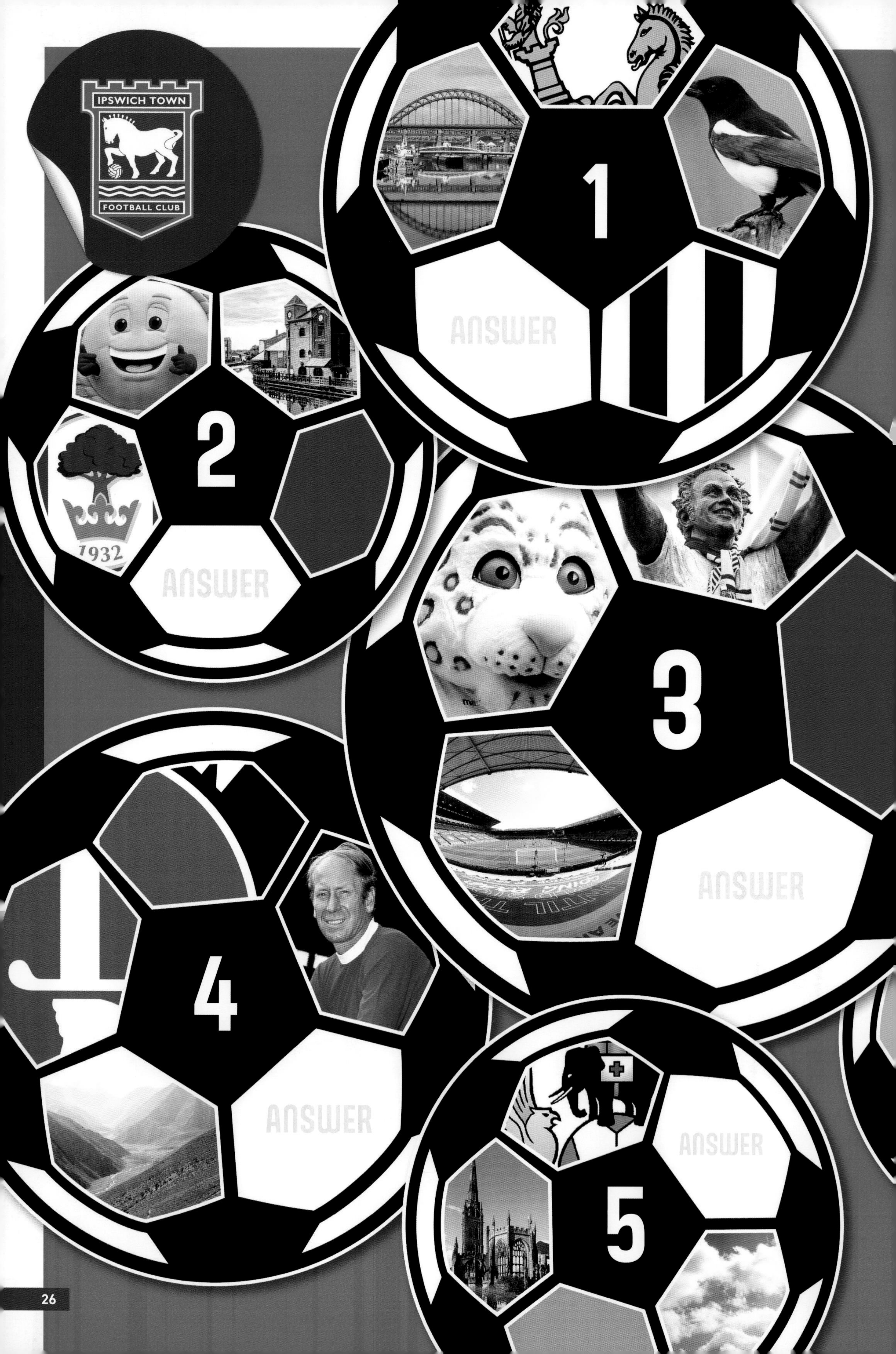
IPSWICH TOWN
FOOTBALL CLUB
1
ANSWER
2
1932
ANSWER
3
ANSWER
4
ANSWER
5
ANSWER

# GUESS THE CLUB

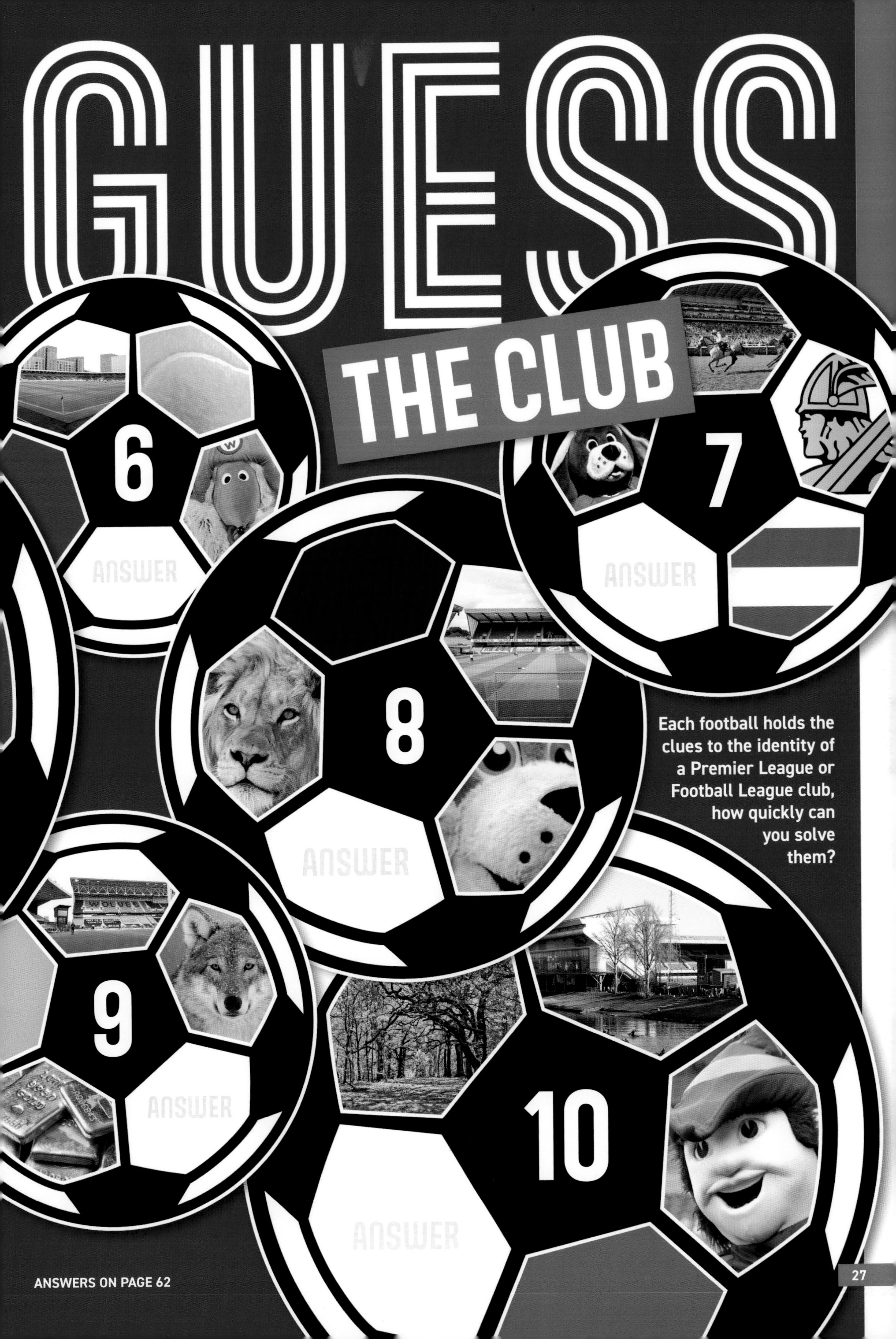


Each football holds the clues to the identity of a Premier League or Football League club, how quickly can you solve them?

ANSWERS ON PAGE 62

# SQUAD 2021/22

## 12 LOUIE BARRY

**POSITION:** Striker

**DOB:** 21 June 2003

**COUNTRY:** England

**Town pulled off a major transfer coup when then they sealed the season-long loan signing of England U18 ace Louie Barry from Aston Villa.**

The former Barcelona youth hot-shot has already featured in the Villa first team, marking his senior debut with a goal in an FA Cup third round tie with Liverpool at Villa Park. He was a key player in Villa's FA Youth Cup winning side last season - operating in a wide attacking role he scored five and assisted four as Villa progressed in the competition before defeating Liverpool in the final.

## 16 IDRIS EL MIZOUNI

**POSITION:** Midfielder

**DOB:** 26 September 2000

**COUNTRY:** Tunisia

**A full Tunisian international, Idris El Mizouni is a technically gifted midfielder who has progressed through the Academy system at Portman Road.**

After earning a first professional contract with the Blues in December 2018, the skillful midfield technician made his Town debut in a 1-1 draw away to Bristol City in March 2019. He has since gained beneficial first team experience with League Two with loans at Cambridge United in 2019/20 and last season with Grimsby Town.

## 18 MACAULEY BONNE

**POSITION:** Striker

**DOB:** 26 October 1995

**COUNTRY:** Zimbabwe

**Ipswich-born Macauley Bonne spent six years with the Blues' Academy between the age of eight and 14 and has returned to Portman Road on a season-long loan from Championship club Queens Park Rangers for the 2021/22 campaign.**

A powerful frontman, Bonne made his professional breakthrough with Colchester United and had successful stints at Leyton Orient and Charlton Athletic before joining Rangers in October 2020.

# 2020/21 FA YOUTH CUP

## A BRIGHT FUTURE BECKONS

**Town fans have always believed the future is blue and white and after witnessing the U18's impressive performances in the 2020/21 FA Youth Cup – the future is clearly a very bright blue and white.**

Under the watchful eye of Academy U18 coach Adem Atay, the young Blues enjoyed an excellent FA Youth Cup campaign as the class of 2021 attempted to emulate the club's successes of 1973, 1975 and 2005 when Town's youngsters secured the most prestigious piece of silverware in youth football.

As a Category Two Academy, at a League One club, Town's bid for FA Youth Cup glory began at the first round stage when they comfortably overcame Southend United 4-1 back on 3 November 2020.

The Town youngster's appetite for goals and glory gathered pace in the second round when they emphatically saw off the challenge of Chelmsford City with a 5-0 away win on 23 November 2020.

Town's reward for a thrilling 3-2 victory over Fulham at Portman Road in the third round on 7 December 2020 was another home tie in round four when Swindon Town were the visitors to Portman Road. Goals from Edwin Agbaje, Ola Bello and Albie Armin saw Town defeat the Robins 3-1 as Atay's team booked a place in the fifth round.

A tough looking fifth round draw saw Town's youngsters make the long haul to Bishop Auckland to face Middlesbrough but a late goal from Armin secured a memorable 1-0 fifth round victory and a place in the quarter-finals.

An eventful quarter-final tie with Sheffield United saw Town edge past the Blades after extra-time. With the scores locked at 2-2, an additional 30 minutes beckoned and saw Town force the visitors into an own goal which secured a 3-2 win and a place in the semi-finals.

Town were handed home advantage for a one-off semi-final meeting with Liverpool as the BT Sport cameras headed to Portman Road on 12 May for a live broadcasting of the game. When Agbaje headed the young Blues in front on the stroke of half-time the dream remained very much alive. Sadly second half goals from Matuesz Musialowski and Melkamu Frauendorf saw the Reds run out 2-1 winners and tee-up a final meeting with Aston Villa.

**Despite falling at the semi-final hurdle, this crop of young players certainly appear to have very promising futures in the game and many have already agreed their first professional contracts with Ipswich Town.**

BRITTON GROUP

# KIERON DYER

**Midfield maestro Kieron Dyer began his career with Ipswich Town and went on to enjoy Premier League fame and international honours with England.**

Born in Ipswich on 29 December 1978, Dyer began his career at Portman Road and made his debut on Boxing Day 1996, just three days before his 18th birthday as Town defeated Crystal Palace 3-1.

Once given a taste of first-team football by boss George Burley, Dyer quickly established himself as one of the top young players in the country. His undoubted ability was rewarded with international recognition with England at U21 level and in 1999 he completed a dream move to the Premier League when he joined Newcastle United for a £6M fee. Another player to enjoy two spells with the club, Dyer played a total of 117 games for Ipswich scoring 12 goals.

# TOWN HEROES

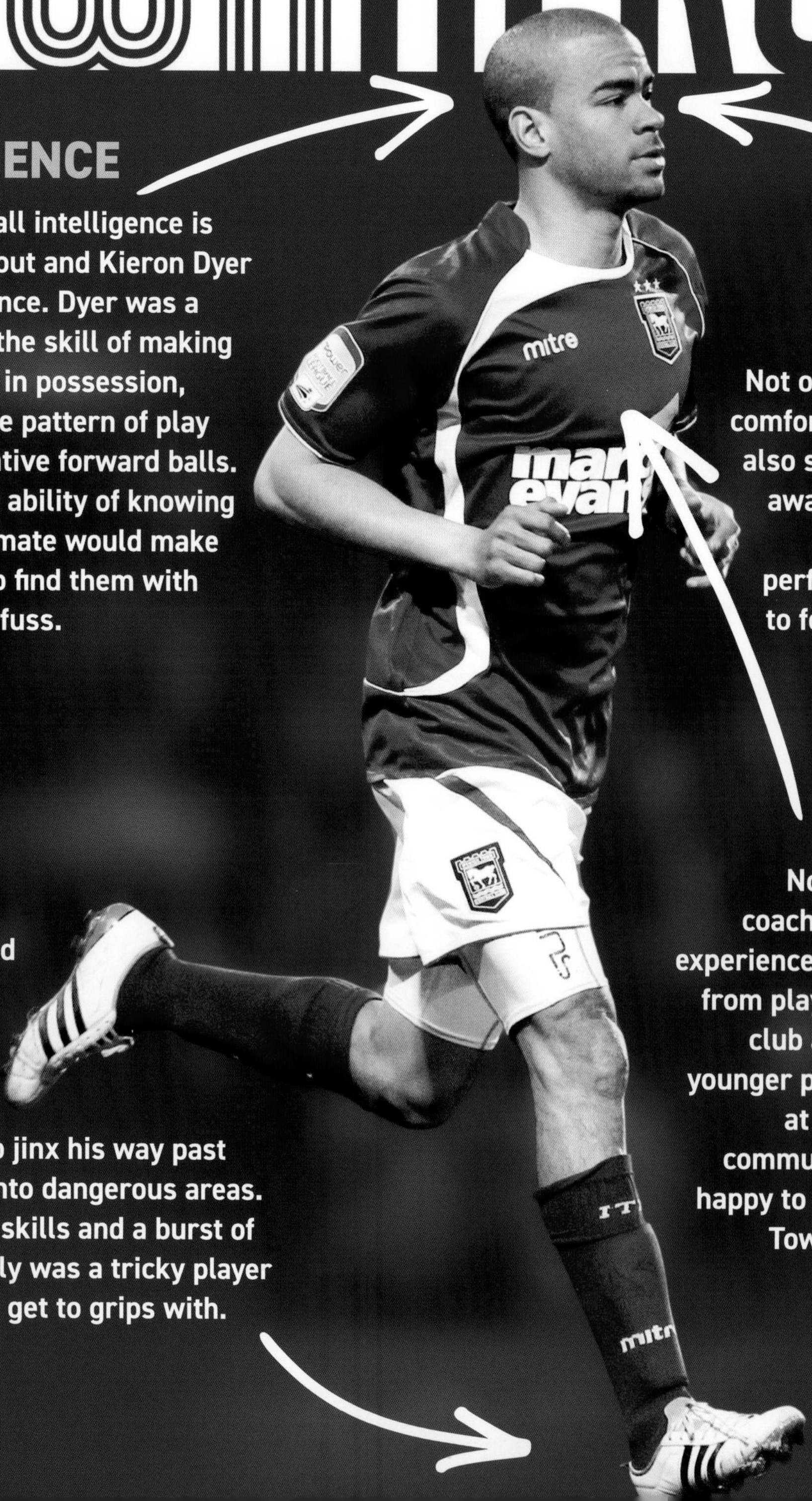

## INTELLIGENCE

A player's football intelligence is often spoken about and Kieron Dyer had it in abundance. Dyer was a player who had the skill of making time for himself in possession, orchestrating the pattern of play and playing creative forward balls. He also had that ability of knowing the runs a teammate would make and the ability to find them with the minimum of fuss.

## EYE FOR AN OPENING

Not only was Dyer extremely comfortable on the ball but he also showed great vision and awareness on the pitch. He appeared to have the perfect eye for a quick pass to feet or a long raking ball forward.

## QUICK FEET

Naturally blessed with exceptional close control and dribbling skills, Dyer had the ability to jinx his way past opponents and into dangerous areas. With such great skills and a burst of speed, Dyer really was a tricky player for opposition to get to grips with.

## ADVICE

Now a member of Town's coaching staff, Dyer uses his experience and knowledge gained from playing at the top level for club and country to help the younger players under his watch at Playford Road. A great communicator, Dyer is always happy to give valuable advice to Town's stars of the future.

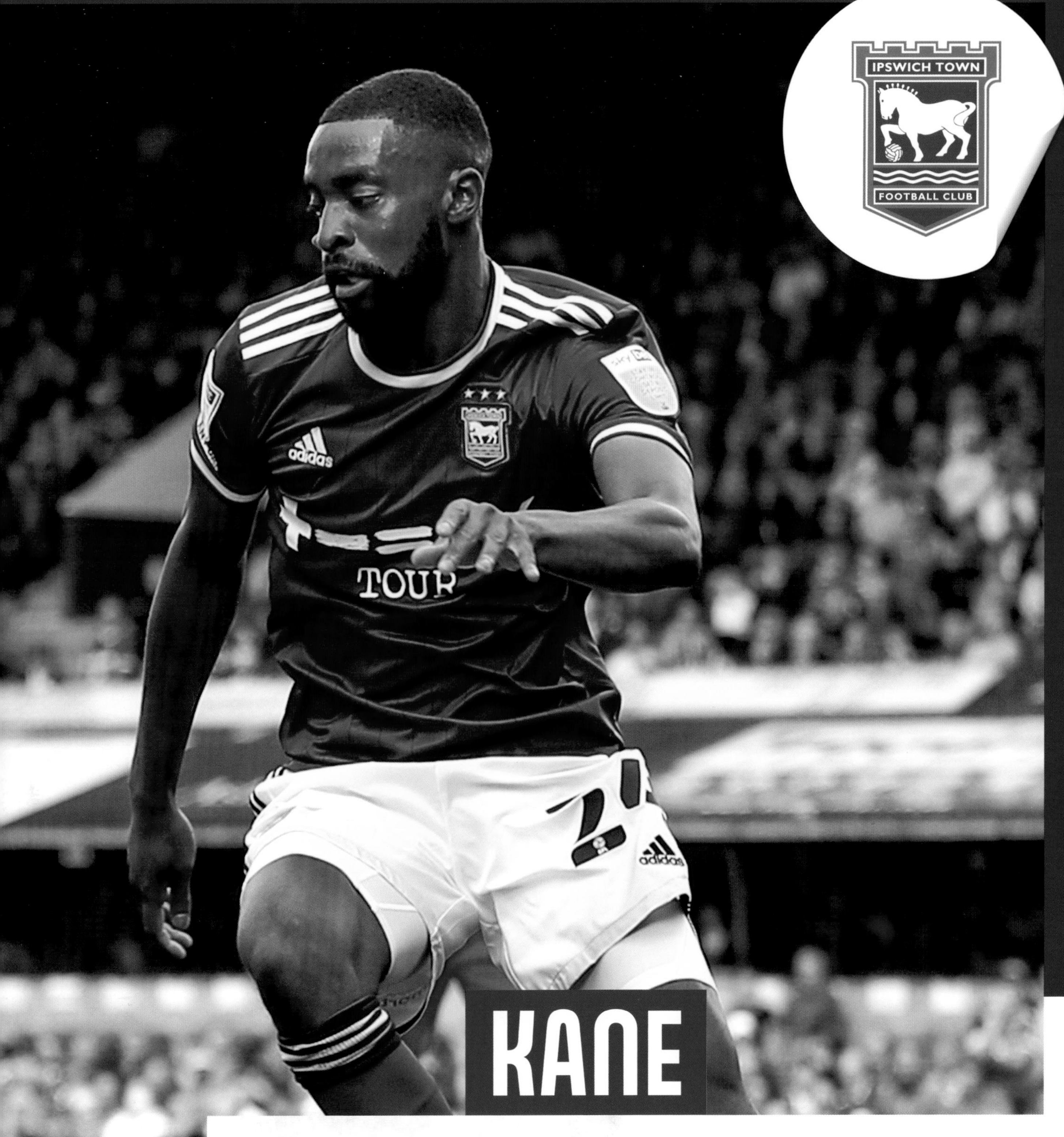


# KANE VINCENT-YOUNG

# TOP GOALSCORER

**Centre forward Ray Crawford tops the Ipswich Town scoring charts having netted an astonishing 227 goals for the Blues.**

Across two spells with Town, Crawford's 227-goal haul is a record that is unlikely to ever be surpassed.

He netted his first goal in a Second Division match away to Swansea back in 1958 and was capped twice by England during his first spell at Portman Road. Unsurprisingly Ray is a member of the club's Hall of Fame.

# MOST INTERNATIONAL CAPS

**Allan Hunter proudly holds the record as Ipswich Town's most capped international player.**

A solid central defender, Hunter made over 350 appearances for Town in an eleven-year career between 1971 and 1982. He won 47 of his 53 caps for Northern Ireland while plying his trade at Portman Road.

An FA Cup winner with Town in 1978, Hunter is also credited with teaching Terry Butcher the art of defending as he progressed through the ranks at Portman Road.

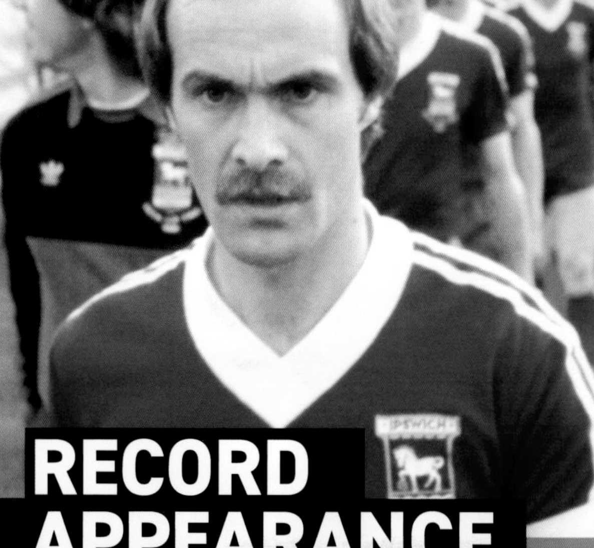

# RECORD APPEARANCE MAKER

**An accomplished defender and born leader, Mick Mills made a record 741 appearances for Ipswich Town.**

Mills was just 17 years old when he made his debut in a 5-2 Portman Road victory over Wolverhampton Wanderers on the final day of the 1965/66 season.

Named captain by Bobby Robson, Mills' Ipswich career saw him skipper the team to FA Cup and UEFA Cup glory in Town's halcyon days. A true club legend, Mills is now the expert summariser for Town's home matches on BBC Radio Suffolk.

# RECORD MAKERS

**A selection of players, games, facts and figures which all shape the club's proud history.**

## RECORD ATTENDANCE

**Town's Portman Road home may well be a 30,311 all-seater stadium now but back in March 1975 a record attendance of 38,010 packed in to witness an FA Cup quarter-final match with Leeds United.**

Despite driving rain, nothing could dampen Ipswich fans' appetite for FA Cup action after seeing Town defeat Wolverhampton Wanderers, Liverpool and Aston Villa to tee-up this quarter-final meeting with the league champions.

The bumper crowd saw a close-fought game end goalless with Town eventually winning through to the semi-final following a 3-2 victory in a third replay.

## YOUNGEST PLAYER

**A powerful academy graduate, striker Connor Wickham took the mantle of becoming Ipswich Town's youngest-ever player when he debuted against Doncaster Rovers in April 2009 aged just 16 years and 11 days.**

Doncaster Rovers were again the opposition when Wickham netted a first professional hat-trick in Town's 6-0 win at the Keepmoat Stadium in February 2011. His form swiftly had Premier League scouts flocking to Portman Road to monitor his growing reputation.

In the summer of 2011 Wickham sealed a move to Sunderland with Town receiving a club record transfer fee.

## 19 KAYDEN JACKSON

**POSITION:** Forward

**DOB:** 22 February 1994

**COUNTRY:** England

**A mobile frontman who joined Ipswich in August 2018 from Accrington Stanley, Kayden Jackson had netted 16 goals in Town colours as at the end of the 2020/21 campaign.**

Following Paul Cook's decision to freshen up the Town strike force with a number of new faces, 27-year-old Jackson will face some stiff competition for a place in the starting line-up in 2021/22. However, with eleven League One goals to his name in Town's 2019/20 season, Jackson has the record of a proven goalscoerer at this level.

## 20 JON NOLAN

**POSITION:** Midfielder

**DOB:** 22 April 1992

**COUNTRY:** England

**All-action midfield maestro Jon Nolan followed his Shrewsbury Town boss Paul Hurst from the New Meadow to Portman Road in August 2018.**

An experienced EFL campaigner, 29-year-old Nolan scored his first goal for Town in a 2-2 Championship draw with Birmingham City a month after his arrival in Suffolk. Liverpool-born Nolan will certainly be looking to make a big impact at Portman Road in Paul Cook's first full season in charge.

# SQUAD 2021/22

## 21 CONOR CHAPLIN

**POSITION:** Striker

**DOB:** 16 February 1997

**COUNTRY:** England

**Conor Chaplin became Ipswich Town's tenth summer signing when he put pen to paper on a three-year deal at Portman Road in July 2021.**

Signed from Barnsley, Chaplin is a versatile front man who helped the Tykes reach the Championship Play-Off semi-finals last season. He began his career at Portsmouth and is certainly well known to Town boss Paul Cook having played under Cook's guidance at Fratton Park.

## 22 TOTO NSIALA

**POSITION:** Defender

**DOB:** 25 March 1992

**COUNTRY:** DR Congo

**Just like teammate Jon Nolan, Toto Nsiala began his career with the Everton Academy before working his way through lower divisions and then joining Ipswich from Shrewsbury Town ahead of the 2018/19 season.**

A fully committed defender, Nsiala has made over half a century of league appearances for the Blues and will look to cement a place in the heart of the Tractor Boys' defence in 2021/22.

# IMPOSSIBLE Footy Decisions

**Would you rather...**

have to play the rest of your football games in 35 degree heat or a blizzard?

**Would you rather...**

have Joe Pigott's ability to score goals or Vaclav Hladky's ability to save them?

**Would you rather...**

have a pause button or a rewind button for your life?

**Would you rather...**

have unlimited battery life on all your devices or free wifi wherever you go?

**Would you rather...**

run 100 laps of the pitch or complete 200 burpees?

**Would you rather...**

score the FA Cup final winning goal against the Canaries in your only game for Ipswich Town or play 300 games for the Blues in League Two?

**Would you rather...**

be remembered for a terrible footy howler or be forgotten completely?

**Would you rather...**

sell your best player to Norwich for £50m or sell him abroad for £20m?

**Would you rather...**

**have to take a penalty against Tomas Holy or have James Norwood take a penalty against you?**

**Would you rather...**

sit right at the back during a game or have the best seats in the stadium, but not be allowed to eat, drink or use the bathroom?

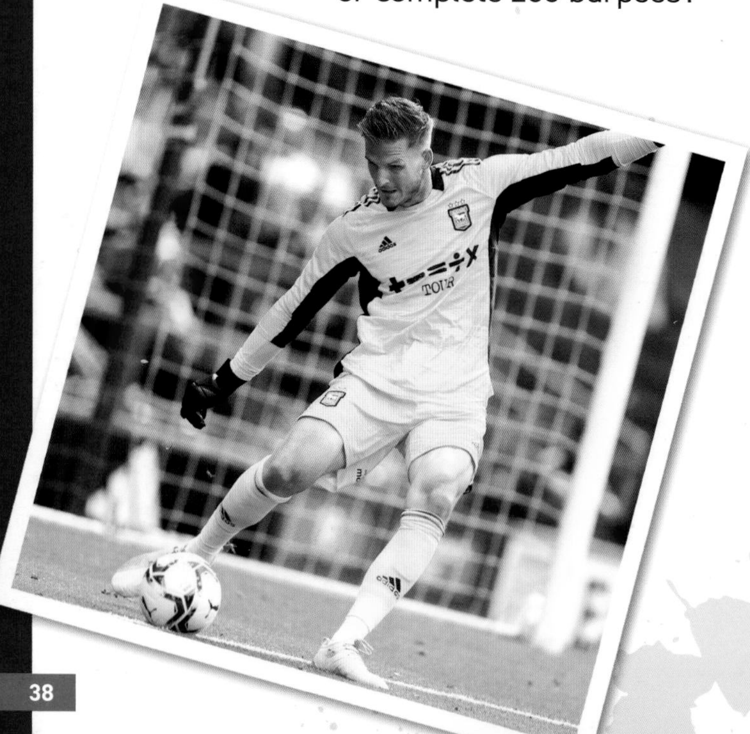

Would you rather...

be the star in League Two or a squad player in the Premier League?

Would you rather...

Ipswich Town win the FA Cup or England win the World Cup?

Would you rather...

your match superstition be wearing the same socks for a season or the same underwear for a month?

Would you rather...

**lose on television or win with nobody watching?**

Would you rather...

have a long, average playing career or have a short, fantastic career cut short by injury?

Would you rather...

lose to Norwich City twice and finish top or beat them twice and finish bottom?

Would you rather...

**clean the dressing room toilet with your toothbrush or the floor with your tongue?**

Would you rather...

play only five minutes for ITFC or win the Premier League with the Canaries?

Would you rather...

have to wear every shirt inside out or every pair of pants backwards?

Would you rather...

**give up your mobile phone for a month or bathing for a month?**

Would you rather...

be alone all your life or surrounded by Norwich City supporters?

Would you rather...

play for Ipswich Town and always lose or sit on the bench and ITFC always win?

Would you rather...

the half-time menu got rid of pies or pop?

Would you rather...

become a legendary manager or a legendary player?

# SCOTT FRASER

**Right-back Mick Mills began his marathon 741-game Ipswich Town career aged just 17 when he made his debut in a 5-2 Second Division victory over Wolverhampton Wanderers in 1966. Over a 16-year period he would go on to write his name in the record books as the club's top appearance maker.**

Town captain Mills became the first, and to-date only, Ipswich Town captain to hold aloft the FA Cup following the Blues' 1-0 Wembley triumph over Arsenal in 1978. As an accomplished defender for one of the country's top league sides and a born leader, Mills won 42 caps for England and also skippered Town to UEFA Cup glory in 1981.

**His 741 games for the club is a total unlikely to ever be surpassed.**

# MICK MILLS

# TOWN HEROES

## TEMPERAMENT

Often faced with containing tricky wingers, Mick Mills had the perfect mindset for defending. He very rarely lost concentration and always kept his cool. In the heat of any on-field duel, Mills kept his mind on the task in hand and was more often than not the winner in one-on-one situations.

## QUICK ON HIS HEELS

Like any defender, Mills was always alive and alert to danger and when it occurred he was quick on his heels to track and tackle opponents. Not only was he swift over the ground but he was also quick to leap and win headed duels too.

## RALLYING CALL

Handed the Town captaincy by Bobby Robson, Mills' ability to lead and inspire his teammates was there for all to see. Always there with an encouraging call to those around him, Mills led by example but was never afraid to let players know if standards had dropped. He really was the perfect leader.

## PASSING SKILLS

Always comfortable with the ball at his feet, Mills was an accomplished ball-playing full-back who could always be relied upon to bring the ball out of defence in a calm fashion and help the side turn defence into attack.

# 1999/2000

**A shirt worn by many of the thousands of Town fans who flocked to Wembley for the 1999/2000 Play-Off final match with Barnsley, this is another kit that brings back fond memories for Town fans.**

Produced by Punch for the third consecutive season, this shirt saw a number of changes from the previous campaign with the club crest reverting from a central position to a more tradition location opposite the manufacturer's logo with the Greene King sponsor's logo below in the centre. The sleeves also changed from white to blue with a white stripe and red flash. There were also white side panels added which ran from the armpit to the bottom of the shirt.

The shorts were all white with a red stripe and carried the Punch logo and club crest on either side. A traditional all-blue sock was topped with a white band and manufacturer's name.

## DRESSED TO IMPRESS

**Of course, most remembered for being the last Town kit to grace Wembley, one of the most memorable fixtures that the Tractor Boys wore this kit for was their incident-packed Play-Off semi-final victory over Bolton Wanderers in May 2000. After suffering a series of Play-Off heartbreaks, it finally came good for Ipswich in an eight-goal thriller that saw Jim Magilton end the night as a hat-trick hero after a sensational 5-3 Town triumph.**

## HE WORE IT WELL

A star performer throughout his Portman Road career, Ipswich captain Matt Holland produced many polished performances in this particular Town strip. After scoring ten goals from midfield in Town's 1999/2000 league campaign, he then skippered the team to Wembley and hoisted aloft the Play-Off trophy following the 4-2 victory over Barnsley in the final.

**Town moved away from the previous season's white sleeved home shirt with a smart, clean, crisp and simple look for the club's 2014/15 Championship campaign.**

With the introduction of a thin black trim to the collar, sleeves and shoulder panel, the shirt carried the three famous Adidas stripes on the sleeves with club crest, manufacturer's logo and club sponsor on the front. Three stars continued to sit above the club crest as an acknowledgement of Town's past successes in the League, FA Cup and UEFA Cup. By this time it had become commonplace for shirts to have competition logos on the sleeves too.

The white shorts had the three Adidas stripes on the sides and also carried the club crest on one side and Adidas logo on the other. The all-blue socks had three white stripes on the top as well as the manufacturer's logo in white on the front.

## DRESSED TO IMPRESS

Town enjoyed an excellent 2014/15 season in the Championship under the shrewd guidance of Mick McCarthy while wearing this strip that many fans now regard as something of an Ipswich classic. They began the campaign with an impressive 2-1 win over Fulham at Portman Road and a performance that really set the tone for the season ahead. An impressive run of form saw Town unbeaten and win eight games from late October to the end of 2014. In and around the Play-Off places throughout the season, they secured sixth spot on the final day of the campaign.

## HE WORE IT WELL

The goals of Republic of Ireland international striker Daryl Murphy really were the driving force behind Town's 2014/15 season. Murphy netted on the opening-day victory over Fulham and went on to net 27 league goals as the division's leading marksman. His prolific goalscoring form saw him voted Town's Player of the Season by the supporters and also the Players' Player of the Season too.

# ALL KITTED OUT

# SQUAD 2021/22

## 23 SONE ALUKO

**POSITION:** Striker

**DOB:** 19 February 1989

**COUNTRY:** Nigeria

**A versatile forward, Sone Aluko agreed a one-year deal at Portman Road on the eve of the new 2020/21 season following his release from Championship club Reading.**

Having played in the Premier League, Championship and Scottish Premier League, 32-year-old Aluko has also plied his trade in the Chinese Super League. After putting pen to paper at Portman Road, the former Nigerian international became the club's twelfth signing of a major summer recruitment drive at Portman Road.

## 24 KANE VINCENT-YOUNG

**POSITION:** Defender

**DOB:** 15 March 1996

**COUNTRY:** England

**A former Tottenham Hotspur Academy player, full-back Kane Vincent-Young joined Town in the summer of 2019 from neighbours Colchester United.**

He made an instant impression at Portman Road and after debuting in a 5-0 victory at Bolton Wanderers in August 2019, he netted his first Ipswich goal in a 1-0 victory over Gillingham a month later. With the ability to power forward and support the attack, Vincent-Young really is the perfect modern-day defender.

## 26 CAMERON BURGESS

**POSITION:** Defender

**DOB:** 21 October 1995

**COUNTRY:** Australia

**Having made his professional debut for Fulham in a match at Ipswich back in August 2014, Portman Road will always hold fond memories for Town central defender Cameron Burgess.**

A highly-rated defender, who was a consistent performer in League One for Stanley last season, Burgess agreed a three-year contract with the Tractor Boys in August 2021 and will add fierce competition for a place in Town's defensive unit.

## 25 TOM CARROLL

**POSITION:** Midfielder

**DOB:** 28 May 1992

**COUNTRY:** England

**A cultured midfield playmaker with an excellent eye for a forward pass, 29-year-old Tom Carroll joined Town in August 2021 with the club's League One campaign already up and running.**

Carroll began his career with Tottenham Hotspur and took in a successful loan spell at Swansea City before completing a permanent move to the South Wales side. He spent the 2020/21 campaign with Queens Park Rangers and as a free agent he then agreed a one-year deal at Portman Road where his impressive range of passing skills should prove of great benefit to the Town squad.

## 27 HAYDEN COULSON

**POSITION:** Defender

**DOB:** 17 June 1998

**COUNTRY:** England

**The 2021/22 campaign was already underway when left-back Hayden Coulson joined Town on a season-long loan deal from Middlesbrough.**

A long-time target for Town boss Paul Cook, Coulson has already taken in one loan spell in East Anglia having spent the second half of the 2018/19 campaign with Cambridge United. An England youth international, Coulson is an attacking full-back whose style appears perfectly suited to Town's 2021/22 League One plans.

IPSWICH TOWN
FOOTBALL CLUB
REKEEM
HARPER

**One of a player's greatest assets is the ability to win the ball. The following exercise can be used to improve a player's tackling abilities.**

# TACKLING

# SOCCER SKILLS

## EXERCISE

Set up a 10m x 20m grid.

**In this two-on-two exercise, the aim of the game is to score a goal by taking the ball past the two opposing defenders, to the end line, and stand on the ball. The defenders just have to stop them.**

As well as producing plenty of opportunities for the defenders to tackle, this session will test the defenders' abilities to work together, and communicate.

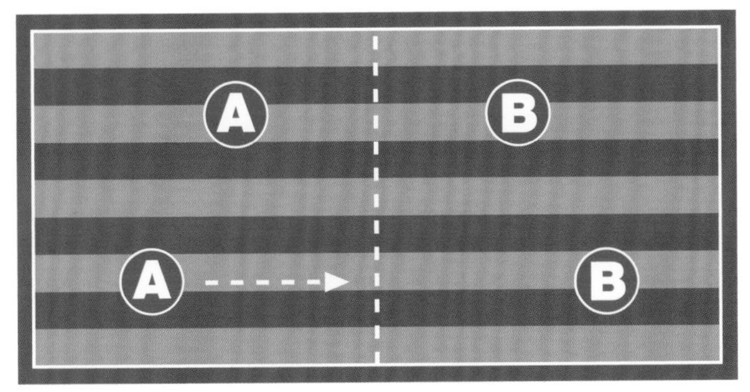

## Key Factors

1. **Be patient - do not dive in.**
2. **Stay on your feet if possible.**
3. **Time the tackle with bodyweight behind it.**
4. **Be determined to win it.**

The reason that great players win so many tackles is not just because they know how to tackle and have good technique, it is because they have big hearts and are determined to win their challenges on the pitch.

# ODD BALLS

Three of the four pictures in each football represent a Premier League or Football League club, can you figure out the football club as well as the odd one out?

1 — A, B, C, D — ANSWER

3 — A, B, C, D — ANSWER

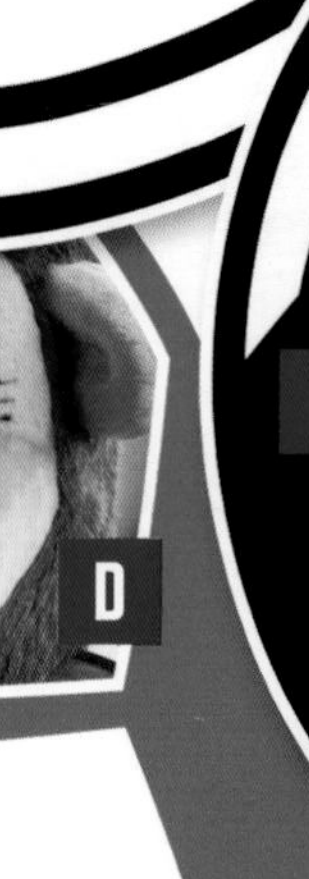

4 — A, B, C, D — ANSWER

ANSWERS ON PAGE 62

6
A
B
C
D
1905
ANSWER
IPSWICH TOWN
FOOTBALL CLUB
7
A
B
C
D
ANSWER
8
A
B
C
D
ANSWER
9
A
B
C
D
FOOTBALL CLUB
ANSWER
10
A
B
C
D
ANSWER

# PAUL MARINER

## 22 MAY 1953 - 9 JULY 2021

**Despite an exciting summer with new players arriving on an almost daily basis and a great deal of optimism surrounding all things Ipswich Town, the club was dealt a devastating blow in July when they learned of the death of one of their greatest-ever players - Paul Mariner.**

After suffering a short battle with brain cancer, Mariner died on 9 July 2021, aged 68.

A true Portman Road legend, Mariner was unquestionably one of the club's greatest-ever centre-forwards and made a huge contribution to Ipswich Town during the most successful era of the club's history.

Signed from Plymouth Argyle by Bobby Robson for a fee of £220,000 back in 1976, Mariner became one of the First Division's most feared frontmen during his Town career.

Part of the Town team that won the FA Cup and the UEFA Cup, his outstanding club form also saw him represent England at the 1982 World Cup finals in Spain.

In total Mariner netted 136 goals for Town in 337 games. For younger supporters who were not fortunate enough to have seen him in action, Paul Mariner was simply the perfect centre-forward, he was powerful and pacy, had a great first touch, an incredible awareness of teammates and a wonderful eye for goal.

Mariner was the Blues' leading marksman with seven goals during the triumphant 1977/78 FA Cup campaign. He got the ball rolling with a second-half brace to see off Second Division Cardiff City in the third round. He then notched his third FA Cup goal of the season as Town eased past Hartlepool United.

His fourth goal of the cup campaign was scored in the 3-0 fifth round replay victory over Bristol Rovers. However, it was at the quarter-final stage he really made his mark on the competition as the England international fired a hat-trick in Town's 6-1 win at Millwall.

After leaving Portman Road, he later played for Arsenal and Portsmouth before plying his trade in Australia, Malta and America. Mariner returned to English football as manager of Plymouth in 2009 and was always a welcome and extremely popular guest whenever he returned to Portman Road.

**The summer of 2021 saw Town make some superb signings as boss Paul Cook set about reshaping the club's playing squad for the 2021/22 League One campaign.**

The influx of new signings has resulted in a host of new names appearing on the back of Town shirts; however the most high-profile signing of this exciting new era at Portman Road appears on the front of the shirts. Throughout the 2021/22 season the club are sponsored by world famous singer and songwriter Ed Sheeran, with the branding for the superstar's latest tour being emblazoned across the front of Town's shirts.

As a favourite son of Suffolk and keen Town fan, the music icon - who is a regular face at Portman Road - was keen to support his local club.

**"The Football Club is a big part of the local community and this is my way of showing my support," Ed told the club website when the sponsorship agreement was announced in May.**

Adding the era-defining artist's name to the front of Town's playing strip has raised the profile of the club all over the globe and has resulted in record sales of the Town shirts for the new season.

In acknowledgement of Ed's continued passionate backing and financial support, the club handed him a place in Paul Cook's squad for the 2021/22 season with the 30-year-old entertainer handed Town's number 17 shirt for the season ahead.

# 17. ED SHEERAN

# LEE EVANS

# COLOUR WES BURNS

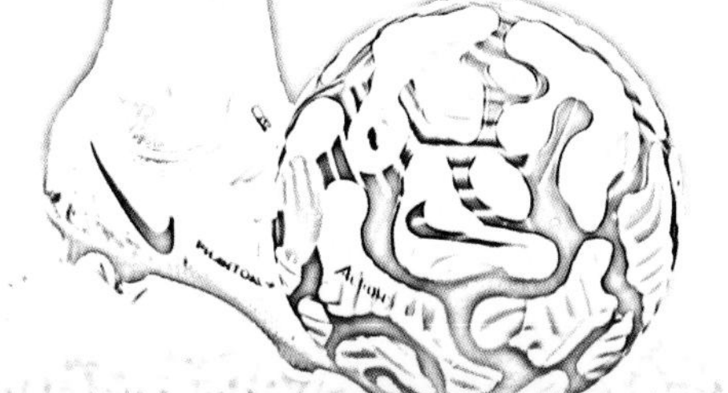

# SQUAD 2021/22

## 28 CHRISTIAN WALTON

**POSITION:** Goalkeeper

**DOB:** 9 November 1995

**COUNTRY:** England

**With the 2021/22 season well underway, Town boss Paul cook strengthened his goalkeeping options with the loan signing of former England U21 international Christian Walton from Brighton & Hove Albion.**

Walton agreed a season-long loan deal at Town just a day before the summer transfer window closed. The 25-year-old stopper is well known to Cook having spent a two-season spell on loan at Wigan Athletic during Cook's reign at the DW Stadium. Walton was a key part of the Latics' side that won the League One title in 2017/18 and that success is sure to serve him and his new teammates well at Portman Road in 2021/22.

## 29 KYLE EDWARDS

**POSITION:** Midfielder

**DOB:** 17 February 1998

**COUNTRY:** England

**Winger Kyle Edwards put pen to paper on a three-year deal with the Blues in August 2021. The 23-year-old joined Town as a free agent following the expiry of his contract at West Bromwich Albion.**

A former teammate of Rekeem Harper at the Hawthorns, Edwards had been with the Baggies since the age of six. He gained great Football League experience with a loan spell at Exeter City in 2017/18 before making 49 first team appearances for Albion.

## 31 VACLAV HLADKY

**POSITION:** Goalkeeper

**DOB:** 14 November 1990

**COUNTRY:** Czech Republic

**Town enhanced their goalkeeping department with the summer signing of Czech stopper Vaclav Hladky from League Two Salford City.**

The 30-year-old 'keeper signed a three-year deal at Portman Road and became the club's fifth summer signing in a busy rebuilding programme ahead of the 2021/22 campaign. Hladky first arrived in the UK in 2019 when he joined St Mirren and spent one season with the Paisley club before trying his luck in England with Salford.

## 43 BERSANT CELINA

**POSITION:** Midfielder

**DOB:** 9 September 1996

**COUNTRY:** Kosovo

**Very much the returning hero, Bersant Celina rejoined Town on the final day of the summer transfer window when he agreed a season-long loan deal from French side Dijon.**

He is already a cult figure with Town fans following a successful spell in Suffolk in 2017/18 when he spent the season on loan from Manchester City. As an attacking midfielder, who loves to try his luck from distance, Celina netted an impressive eight goals in 38 appearances for Town during his first spell at the club.

## 44 JANOI DONACIEN

**POSITION:** Defender

**DOB:** 3 November 1993

**COUNTRY:** St Lucia

**A versatile defender, Janoi Donacien initially joined the Blues on loan from Accrington Stanley in the summer of 2018 before making the move a permanent arrangement in the 2019 January transfer window.**

Primarily operating at right-back during his first two seasons at Town, Donacien spent last season on loan at Fleetwood Town and will now look to show new Town boss Paul Cook what he is capable of having returned to his parent club.

## 55 SAM MORSY

**POSITION:** Midfielder

**DOB:** 10 September 1991

**COUNTRY:** Egypt

**Defensive midfielder Sam Morsy became Town's 19th and final new signing of the 2021 summer transfer window when he arrived at Portman Road from Middlesbrough on 31 August 2021.**

The Egyptian international began his career at Port Vale before then first playing for Paul Cook at Chesterfield and then at Wigan Athletic. With over 400 first team career games to his name, Morsy will bring experience and tenacious ball-winning skills to the Blues' midfield.

Can you identify these six Town legends from the clues given? Good luck!

# GUESS WHO

## 1. WHO AM I?

I began my playing career with Middlesbrough

I joined Town in 1995

I was signed by Ipswich from Celtic

I was on the scoresheet in the Blues' 1999/2000 Play-Off triumph at Wembley

I had a brief spell as the club's caretaker-manager

## 2. WHO AM I?

I was born in Suffolk

I made my Town debut back in 1973

I scored a total of nine league goals for Ipswich

I'm famed for scoring a historic goal in Town's history

I played over 200 league games for Colchester United later in my career

## 3. WHO AM I?

I initially came to Ipswich on loan

I marked my Town debut with a goal

I was leading scorer when Town reached the Championship Play-Offs in 2014/15

I played international football for the Republic of Ireland

I left Town in a big money move in 2016

I joined the Blues in 2014

I was signed from Notts County

I was signed by Mick McCarthy

I was voted Town's Player of the Season on three occasions

I left the club in the summer of 2019

## 4. WHO AM I?

I was handed my Ipswich Town debut by Bobby Robson

I marked my debut with a goal

I was part of the club's 1991/92 Second Division title-winning team

I won England U21 caps while at Town

I had two spells as a player at Portman Road

## 5. WHO AM I?

## 6. WHO AM I?

I was born in Ipswich in 1978

I made my first team debut for Town as a teenager

I left Ipswich for a then club record fee in 1999

I returned to Town on loan in 2011

I'm currently helping coach Ipswich's stars of the future

ANSWERS ON PAGE 62

# BARTOSZ BIALKOWSKI

Popular Polish goalkeeper Bartosz Bialkowski completed a hat-trick of Ipswich Town Player of the Season awards when he was voted the Blues' top performer in 2017/18. Although John Wark has won the award on four occasions, only Bialkowski was been presented with the award in three consecutive seasons.

The 6ft 4in stopper joined Town on an initial two-year deal in the summer of 2014 from Notts County and played a starring role as Mick McCarthy's men reached the end-of-season Play-Offs.

An excellent shot stopper who always gave real confidence to those playing in front of him, Bialkowski made 178 appearances for Town before joining Millwall in 2019.

# TOWN HEROES

## VOICE

Charged with organising the defensive unit in front of him, goalkeeper Bartosz Bialkowski would often be heard barking instructions to his teammates. With the whole pitch in his sight it is an important part of the goalkeeper's role to advise teammates of the dangers he can spot.

## EYES

Always keeping a close eye on the ball, goalkeeper Bialkowski used his sight to judge the flight of crosses and the speed of shots heading his way. Viewing a situation and making an instant judgement is such a vital part of goalkeeping - particularly when quickly assessing whether to come for a ball or leave it for a defender.

## RIGHT ARM

Not only will goalkeepers use their arms when diving to make saves and collect crosses but also once in possession of the ball 'keepers can of course quickly bowl the ball out to start attacks. Bialkowski often used a combination of quick thinking and a strong arm to bowl the ball forward and help the Blues spring an attack.

## HANDS

Blessed with the ability to quickly bring his hands into action to repel opposition's efforts on goal, Bialkowski could always be relied upon to pull off saves and use his hands effectively to either gather the ball or push it to safety.

# JOE PIGOTT

# FAST FORWARD»

Do your predictions for 2021/22 match our own?...

**LEAGUE ONE WINNERS**

Ipswich Town

**LEAGUE ONE TOP SCORER**

Macauley Bonne

**LEAGUE ONE RUNNERS-UP**

MK Dons

**LEAGUE ONE PLAY-OFF WINNERS**

Sunderland

**FA CUP WINNERS**

Brighton & Hove Albion

**FA CUP RUNNERS-UP**

Leeds United

**LEAGUE CUP WINNERS**

Arsenal

**LEAGUE CUP RUNNERS-UP**

Leicester City

**PREMIER LEAGUE WINNERS**

Manchester United

**PREMIER LEAGUE RUNNERS-UP**

Chelsea

**PREMIER LEAGUE TOP SCORER**

Anthony Martial

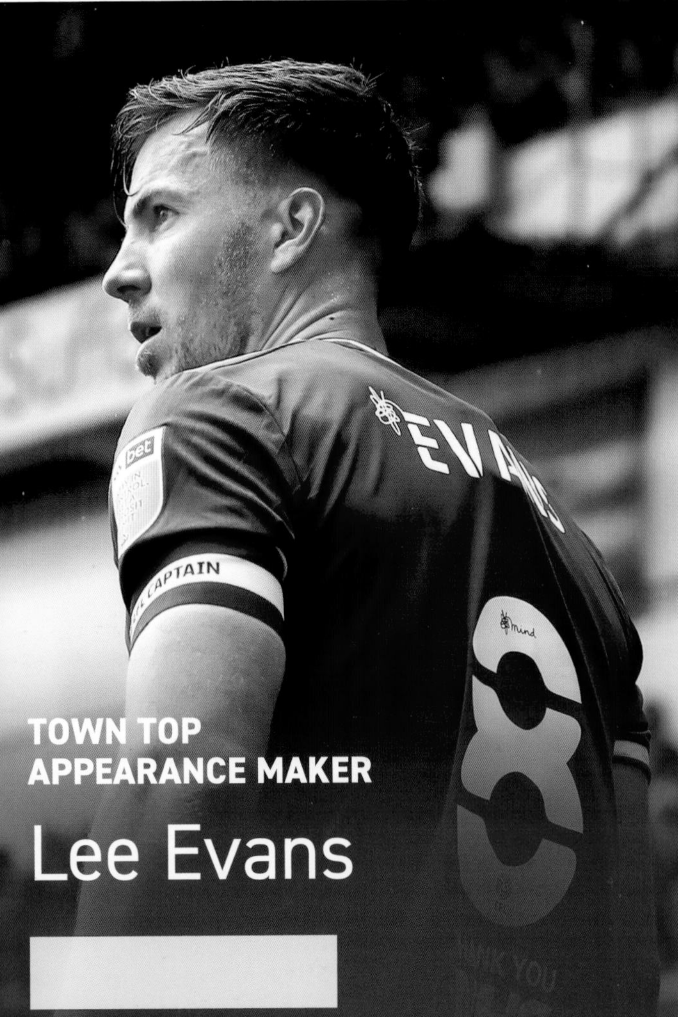

**TOWN TOP APPEARANCE MAKER**

Lee Evans

**TOWN PLAYER OF THE YEAR**

Joe Pigott

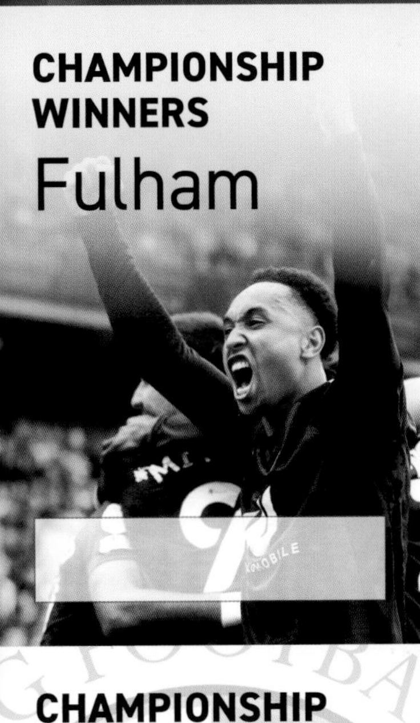

**CHAMPIONSHIP WINNERS**

Fulham

**CHAMPIONSHIP RUNNERS-UP**

Derby County

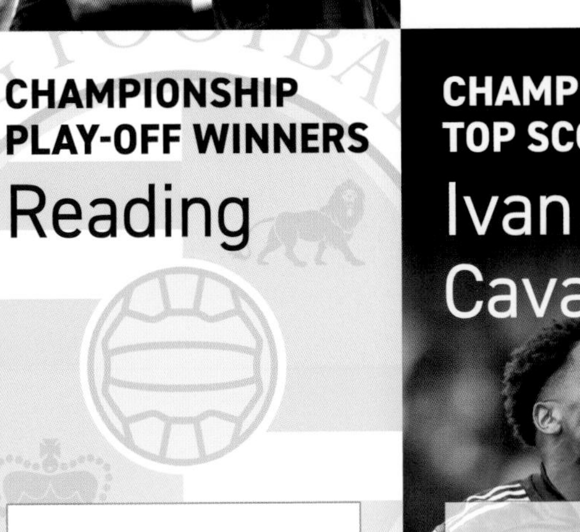

**CHAMPIONSHIP PLAY-OFF WINNERS**

Reading

**CHAMPIONSHIP TOP SCORER**

Ivan Cavaleiro

# ANSWERS

## PAGE 11
## SOCCER SEARCH

Bicycle Kick.

## PAGE 14
## CLASSIC FANTASTIC

## PAGE 26
## GUESS THE CLUB

1. Newcastle United. 2. Wigan Athletic. 3. Leeds United. 4.Charlton Athletic. 5. Coventry City. 6. AFC Wimbledon. 7. Doncaster Rovers. 8. Millwall. 9.Wolverhampton Wanderers. 10. Nottingham Forest.

## PAGE 48
## ODD BALLS

1. Sunderland, C. 2. Portsmouth, C. 3. Arsenal, B. 4. Crewe Alexandra, A. 5. Queens Park Rangers, C. 6. Crystal Palace, B. 7. MK Dons, B. 8. Reading, B. 9. Birmingham City, C. 10. West Ham United, D.

## PAGE 56
## GUESS WHO?

1. Tony Mowbray. 2. Roger Osborne. 3. Daryl Murphy. 4. Bartosz Bialkowski. 5. Jason Dozzell. 6. Kieron Dyer.